MW00565288

Fierce Departures
The Poetry of Dionne Brand

Fierce Departures
The Poetry of Dionne Brand

Selected
with an
introduction by
Leslie C. Sanders
and an
afterword by
Dionne Brand

LAURIER POETRY SERIES

Wilfrid Laurier University Press

We acknowledge the support of the Canada Council for the Arts for our publishing program. We acknowledge the financial support of the Government of Canada through the Book Publishing Industry Development Program for our publishing activities.

Library and Archives Canada Cataloguing in Publication

Brand, Dionne, 1953–
    Fierce departures : the poetry of Dionne Brand / selected with an introduction by Leslie C. Sanders ; and an afterword by Dionne Brand.

(Laurier poetry series)
Includes bibliographical references.
ISBN 978-1-55458-038-5

    i. Sanders, Leslie Catherine, 1944–   ii. Title.   iii. Series: Laurier poetry series

PS8553.R275F54 2009   C811'.54   C2008-907328-2

© 2009 Wilfrid Laurier University Press
Waterloo, Ontario, Canada N2L 3C5
www.wlupress.wlu.ca

Cover image: *100* Drawings for Hanneline, /27* (2008), by Nell Painter. Reproduced courtesy of the artist. Cover design and text design by P.J. Woodland.

Table of Contents

Foreword

At the beginning of the twenty-first century, poetry in Canada—writing and publishing it, reading and thinking about it—finds itself in a strangely conflicted place. We have many strong poets continuing to produce exciting new work, and there is still a small audience for poetry; but increasingly, poetry is becoming a vulnerable art, for reasons that don't need to be rehearsed.

But there are things to be done: we need more real engagement with our poets. There needs to be more access to their work in more venues—in classrooms, in the public arena, in the media—and there needs to be more, and more different kinds, of publications that make the wide range of our contemporary poetry more widely available.

The hope that animates this series from Wilfrid Laurier University Press is that these volumes help to create and sustain the larger readership that contemporary Canadian poetry so richly deserves. Like our fiction writers, our poets are much celebrated abroad; they should just as properly be better known at home.

Our idea is to ask a critic (sometimes herself a poet) to select thirty-five poems from across a poet's career; write an engaging, accessible introduction; and have the poet write an afterword. In this way, we think that the usual practice of teaching a poet through eight or twelve poems from an anthology is much improved upon; and readers in and out of classrooms will have more useful, engaging, and comprehensive introductions to a poet's work. Readers might also come to see more readily, we hope, the connections among, as well as the distances between, the life and the work.

It was the ending of an Al Purdy poem that gave Margaret Laurence the epigraph for *The Diviners*: "but they had their being once/and left a place to stand on." Our poets still do, and they are leaving many places to stand on. We hope that this series helps, variously, to show how and why this is so.

—*Neil Besner*
General Editor

Biographical Note

Born in Guayguayare, Trinidad, on January 7, 1953, Dionne Brand moved to Canada in 1970. She settled in Toronto, where she attended the Ontario Institute for Studies in Education at the University of Toronto, completing her M.A. and doctoral coursework. Brand has held several university positions: at the University of Guelph, at St. Lawrence University in upstate New York, and at Simon Fraser University, where she held the Ruth Wynn Woodward Chair in Women's Studies. She holds a university research chair and is a professor in the School of English and Theatre Studies at the University of Guelph.

Brand's oeuvre is considerable: nine volumes of poetry, three novels, a collection of short stories, two collections of essays, three documentary films, a variety of occasional essays, stories, and scholarly pieces, and two collections of oral history. Her work is widely read, anthologized, and taught, both in North America and the Caribbean, and is also well known in Europe. *At the Full and Change of the Moon* and *What We All Long For* have been translated into Italian, and the latter into German. There is also an Italian/English bilingual anthology of her poetry, *Luce Ostinata*. In Canada, Brand has received many awards, notably the Governor General's Award for Poetry and the Trillium Award (for *Land to Light On*, 1997), the Pat Lowther Award (for *thirsty*, 2005), the City of Toronto Book Award (for *What We All Long For*, 2006) and the Harbourfront Festival Award (2006), given in recognition of her substantial contribution to literature. *No Language Is Neutral* and *Inventory* were shortlisted for the Governor General's Award for Poetry, and *In Another Place, Not Here* was shortlisted for the Chapters/Books in Canada First Novel Award and the Trillium Award and was cited by the *New York Times* as one of its one hundred best books of the year. *thirsty* was nominated for the City of Toronto Book Award and the Griffin Prize. The *Los Angeles Times* chose Brand's novel, *At the Full and Change of the Moon*, as one of the one hundred best books of the year.

Introduction

Dionne Brand's writing charts a complex history, a resolute politics, an ethics of witness, and the occasional hopefulness wedded to deep despair. The long poem is Dionne Brand's form, and so this anthology invites its readers to return these excerpts to their sources: *No Language Is Neutral* (1990, 1998), *Land to Light On* (1997), *thirsty* (2002), *Inventory* (2006). The poems selected here provide a distillation of Brand's poetic concerns and follow the trajectory of her changing vision. Her voice always locates itself in particular places, histories, and social relations, and is never abstract. Her poetry meditates on the history that produced her, and how it inflects and complicates rootedness and belonging, whether in the Caribbean of her birth or in Canada, where she has settled. Yet, as profoundly as Brand maps the migrations of the African diaspora, following the contours of her own history from the Caribbean to Canada, she then moves beyond migratory binaries of home and "not-home" and the emotional diasporic genealogy of origins. First, in *thirsty*, she concerns herself with how Toronto's diverse inhabitants produce the place to which they have come, and then, in *Inventory*, with how inhumanity and grace are everywhere located.

Ironically, Brand's focus on location is also considered a distinctly Canadian question: Where is here? In Brand's mouth, however, the question is quite different from that posed by Northrop Frye. For the African diaspora, descendents of those who passed through the Door of No Return into the hell of New World slavery, the question resonates with pain, loss, dislocation, and deep ambivalence about place. Whereas for immigrants and refugees, the New World historically has signalled new beginnings, painful histories erased or escaped, for those who came in chains, history is a haunting:

> Hard-bitten on mangrove and wild
> bush, the sea wind heaving any remnants of
> consonant curses into choking aspirate. No
> language is neutral seared in the spine's unravelling.
> Here is history too.... The malicious horizon made us the
> essential thinkers of technology. How to fly gravity,
> how to balance basket and prose reaching for

murder. Silence done curse god and beauty here,
people does hear things in this heliconia peace
a morphology of rolling chain and copper gong
now shape this twang, falsettos of whip and air
rudiment this grammar. Take what I tell you. When
these barracks held slaves between their stone
halters, talking was left for night and hush was idiom
and hot core. (*No Language Is Neutral*, 20)

In Brand's poetry, landscape teems with the history that has taken place
within it, and is marked by it. The preceding passage, from the eponymous
poem of Dionne Brand's *No Language Is Neutral*, samples the continual con-
versation in her poetry between figure and ground, person and place. The
phrase is borrowed from Derek Walcott's "Midsummer," but Brand deploys it
in opposition to his ambivalent relation to Africa and England, the cultures
that have produced him. Walcott writes: "No language is neutral; / the green
oak of English is a murmurous cathedral / where some took umbrage, some
peace, but every shade, / all, helped to widen its shadow." In Brand's world,
however, there is neither peace nor shade, only bitter history barely written,
and when written at all, neither by women, nor about them (Gingell, 52). The
speaker addresses her great-grandmother:

History will only hear you if you give birth to a
woman who smoothes starched linen in the wardrobe
drawer, trembles when she walks and who gives birth
to another woman who cries near a river and
vanishes and who gives birth to a woman who is a
poet, and, even then. (*No Language Is Neutral*, 23)

The poet's task, then, is to render this history palpable, trace its inscription
in and through personal narrative in order to unfold its wider significance.
Although most of the volume to which this poem is central is set in Trinidad,
the poem itself moves from Trinidad to Toronto, recounting the speaker's first
migration as well as her returning visit. Her migration to Toronto repeats
others: her sister before her, her mother (to England) before them. Encap-
sulated in the collection *No Language Is Neutral* is family and personal history
that descends from slave barracks and dreams of flight, flight's recurrence
laden by palimpsests of bondage.

The poem speaks two languages, what Brand called, in an interview with
Makeda Silvera, "Received Standard" and "Trinidadian," each language critical
to the poem's precision of thought and expression. "Silence done curse god and

beauty here, / people does hear things in this heliconia peace / a morphology of rolling chain and copper gong / now shape this twang ..." A mark for Brand of her poetic maturity, this effortless bilingualism is an exact perspective, a counter-rhythm, an oppositional beat. History resides in language, which in turn inscribes it on to landscape, translating space and place into lived genealogy (Silvera, 368).

In the first part of "No language is neutral," Trinidadian renders family history vividly intimate. However, migration, although necessary, impoverishes and strips the speaker of context, and also language: "This city, / mourning the smell of flowers and dirt, cannot tell / me what to say even if it chokes me. Not a single / word drops from my lips for twenty years about living / here." The language of the city is stark and simple, unmodified nouns, short simple words, fewer of the poet's characteristic sentences that sweep the reader along, clause after clause, in waves of language. Space is hostile, place must be created: "I walk Bathurst Street until it come like home," the poet recalls about Christmas at Pearl's. Safe haven must be simulated "with the blinds drawn," yet "even / our nostalgia was a lie, skittish as the truth these / bundle of years." In striking contrast to the deep connection to place in the opening sections of "no language is neutral," connection to place in Toronto is tenuous: "Dumbfounded I walk as if these sidewalks are a / place I'm visiting"—and Trinidadian sounds tentative, in contrast to its precise disclosure of idea and tenderness in the earlier sections of the poem.

This collection startles with its range of emotion: from searing to tender, from whiplash to passionate caress. It constitutes the poet's poetic "coming out," her declaration of her love for a woman, women. Yet, as in all Brand's work, the intensely personal is deeply informed by the politics that surround: the poet records: "always fear of a woman watching the world from an / evening beach with her sister, the courage between / them to drink a beer and assume their presence against the coral chuckle of male voices. In / another place, not here, a woman might ..." Thus the freedom arising from recognition of self in a place, and in another, is constrained by hostile gaze and bitter legacy.

Yet the poem does not remain trapped between home and exile. It moves from "here" and "there" to "another place, not here," a phrase of deferral that signals the diaspora's continual condition and also its hope; for a diasporic consciousness, by definition, imagines itself rooted in an elsewhere, or believes that rootedness, and so safety, is elsewhere possible. Yet, as her later work will clarify, Brand eschews the romance of origin and homeland. "Map to the Door of No Return" she titles her 2001 meditation on the condition of those flung into the West by slavery, a reference to the House of Slaves on the Île de Gorée in Senegal, now a memorial to the millions shipped from Africa's west coast to the plantations of the New World. "Each sentence realised or / dreamed jumps like a pulse with history and takes a / side," "no language is neutral" insists, its account-ing of an unspoken history giving voice to a narrative both intimate and epical. *No Language Is Neutral* constitutes a powerful intervention into histories of slavery, colonialism, independence, migration. For all its ambivalence concerning place and possibility, the poem resolves in a coming to self and voice: the collection's final sentences are: "They say this place / does not exist, then, my tongue is mythic. I was here / before."

Land to Light On revisits the locations of *No Language Is Neutral*, this time in a reversed sequence. Where the earlier volume had taken Trinidad as its starting point, resting only tentatively in Canada, *Land to Light On,* in the section included here (also called "Land to Light On") and in the collection itself, begins in "this land," Canada, and the literalness of land, soil, space, is the focus of the poet's interrogation: "Maybe this wide country just stretches your life to a thinness / just trying to take it in." Salient is the connection between land, language and history; in poem *V i*, the "where is here" is not only a matter of geography but of mapping a history, which requires finding a language, "guess[ing] at the fall of words." In contrast to the intimacy with the Trinidadian landscape in the earlier work, in this seeking to make connection, the speaker is buffeted by the land's very vastness and its heady winds. The view is bird's eye, the volume's title itself evoking the migration of birds, their need to alight and the impermanence of their stay. The next poem in the sequence returns to Trinidad, "your house behind your eyebrows," but perspective in the poem shifts. By its conclusion, place is identified by its mapping, not its landscape. It is the poet's relation to place that is undergoing revision in this volume. The change, ultimately, is renunciation: "I am giving up land to light on," the next poem announces.

What can that mean? In that one phrase is jettisoned an entire language of home and exile, belonging and unbelonging, nation and citizenship. The reason, woven through the restive detailing of land and its mappings, arises out of a profound understanding of the implications of belonging's claims. "[E]verywhere you walk on the earth there's harm, / everywhere resounds," the poet observes. There is land and sky and there is history in Brand's poetics of landscape. "[S]ky was a doorway" for slaves longing for freedom: nature, implacable and without volition, brings relief from the harm that is willed and results from human action. Moreover, slaves flying back to Africa people the folklore of the enslaved of the Caribbean and North America. Only sky encompassed both their place of bondage and their homeland. The poet's bird-like flight again is a palimpsest. In her renunciation of land and country, the poet discloses the commitment that she believes acceptance entails: "I'm giving up on land to light on, and why not, / I can't perfect my own shadow, my violent sorrow, my / individual wrists." These lines suggest that the ethical relation implied by the converse, embracing of place, nation, citizenship, is one of total responsibility. The turning away, the refusal, is not then simply a denial of connection but an acknowledgement of individual limits and an unwillingness to live up to the demands of belonging as they are usually construed, while at the same time indicating what commitment would involve.

If *No Language Is Neutral* moves painfully between "home" and "exile," and *Land to Light On* turns from identification with country, *thirsty* establishes a new relation with place and takes up the question "where is here" in a new fashion. In *thirsty*, the poet contemplates Toronto as "the city / that's never happened before." *thirsty's* Toronto, both literal and a sign of possibility, replete with "cramped dirt," "broken / air," "sweet ugliness," is a striking contrast to the vistas and lush landscapes of the earlier volumes. *thirsty* writes the city in several registers. At the core is the story of Alan and his family. Based on the murder of the Jamaican immigrant Albert Johnson in 1979, shot by police during a domestic call, Alan's dying ("XII") and its impact on his mother Chloe, his wife Julia, and his daughter constitutes the volume's narrative. Two poems here depict the family's shattering: "XII," Alan's death, and "XVIII," in which "two women," Julia and Chloe, watch their daughter ride off on her bicycle. Their poignant yearning for the daughter is expressed as an amalgam of enduring hope and crippling sorrow. The poem's alternating lines, long and short, mirror their expansive and constricting emotions. The unnamed daughter's receding figure evokes the inevitable generational divide, the second generation's life and world, to the first generation unknowable.

In the next poem included in this anthology, the poet/narrator, an inhabitant of the city like all the others, reflects on her own relation to these events: "I don't remember that frail morning, how / could I?" The narrator's commentary works on two levels. As city denizen, she mulls over her responsibility, recognizing what she has in common with Alan: "thirst" "falling," although "busy with my own life," her ignorance of the tragedy is understandable. The meanings are both ironic and not; there is a factuality about the tone that begs for humanity, ethical concern, political action. The ethics of human community waft through the poem, are considered, reverberate accusingly.

thirsty's third register is the poetic eye and voice: painterly, descriptive, observant, unjudgmental, tender and full of love for the city and its inhabitants who have come from all over the world, thirsty. In this register, *thirsty*, then, takes up the issue of ethical citizenship afresh. "Look it's like this, I'm just like the rest, / limping across the city, flying when I can," the poet demurs.

Yet the collection as a whole belies this modest claim by making of the city and its thirsty newcomers a vision of possibility.

In *Inventory*, however, hopefulness is gone. In the selection published here, the first half of poem "III," the poet observes "she" who sits by the television weeping at the heart-wrenching human toll of the war in Iraq and carnage elsewhere. The litany of death also serves to counteract and reprove the culture of violence that makes of the "real" and the representational a continuum: "the news was advertisement for movies, / the movies were the real killings." The questions of human relation, responsibility, ethical belonging, so vivid in earlier texts, are in this poem on the level of the speaking voice, withered by fear and paranoia. The boundaries between the speaker, she and the lives of those she sees through the television's window blur. The reader, the poem's "you," is invited in intimate address, to share the speaker's respite in music and the sea, the watcher becoming protector: "sleep while I keep watch, / know that I am your spy here, your terrorist, / find me." The irregularity of stanzas evokes the speaker's frantic grief and terror, and nouns and noun clauses pile up like the bodies they inventory. In a later part of this poem, the speaker proposes more calmly: "'let's at least admit we mean each other / harm, / we intend to do damage' // then she may stop this vigil" (42). But of course she cannot do so, finishing the poem, "... eight hundred every month / for the last year, and one hundred / and twenty in a brutal four days, / things, things add up" (52).

In contrast to the specificity of *thirsty*'s location, in *Inventory*, when the speaker names her location, she is a traveller: Egypt in one poem, Miami airport in another, and Italy in a third. Otherwise the speaker does not place herself geographically. The central poem in *Inventory*, the first part of which is included here, begins in front of the television, which, as Diana Brydon observes, renders the entire world accessible and immediate, and so reconfigures social relations (Brydon, 1002). As in *thirsty*, in these poems an ethics of relation is probed, performed, simultaneously failed and affirmed. The powerful voice of *Inventory* haunts: "my job," the poet concludes at the end of the collection, "is to revise and revise this bristling list, / hourly" (*Inventory*, 100).

I began by suggesting a coincidence between Brand's question Where is here? and that of Northrop Frye as a point of departure, emphasizing the differences in their responses and in the very resonances of the question. This coincidence is also juxtaposition and conjunction, for Brand's work constitutes a profound intervention into the national poetic imaginary. In all her work—the entire corpus of her poetry, as well as her novels, short stories, and essays—Brand scrutinizes the implications of her figurative self on Canadian ground. Canada's presence in her writing comprises a sustained dialogue with that national space, rewriting its contours and widening its exclusionary focus to encompass its present, illuminate aspects of its past, and propose its future. Brand's work comprises a yoking of histories and imaginaries, a broadening of understanding.

As poet, then, Dionne Brand moves beyond the particular history of slavery and colonialism, migration and a hunger for belonging, to a broader questioning of relation to place and society. Her searing language decries the inhumanities that deform the lives of individuals and communities and bring nation into question. The helplessness and despair so frequent in Brand's work arise out of the demands the poet makes first and foremost of herself, as citizen "like any other" in both the place and the wider world in which she lives.

—Leslie C. Sanders

Bibliography

Brand, Dionne. *No Language Is Neutral.* Toronto: Coach House Press, 1990; rev. ed. McClelland & Stewart, 1998.

——. *Land to Light On.* Toronto: McClelland & Stewart, 1997.

——. *Map to the Door of No Return: Notes to Belonging.* Toronto: Doubleday Canada, 2001.

——. *thirsty.* Toronto: McClelland & Stewart, 2002.

——. *Inventory.* Toronto: McClelland & Stewart, 2006.

Brydon, Diana. "Dionne Brand's Global Intimacies: Practising Affective Citizenship," *University of Toronto Quarterly* 76.3 (2007): 990–1006.

Gingell, Susan. "Returning to Come Forward: Dionne Brand Confronts Derek Walcott," *Journal of West Indian Literature* 6.2 (May 1994): 43–53.

Silvera, Makeda. "Dionne Brand: In the Company of My Work." In Makeda Silvera, ed., *The Other Woman: Women of Colour in Contemporary Canadian Literature,* 356–80. Toronto: Sister Vision, 1995.

No language is neutral. I used to haunt the beach at
Guaya, two rivers sentinel the country sand, not
backra white but nigger brown sand, one river dead
and teeming from waste and alligators, the other
rumbling to the ocean in a tumult, the swift undertow
blocking the crossing of little girls except on the tied
up dress hips of big women, then, the taste of leaving
was already on my tongue and cut deep into my
skinny pigeon toed way, language here was strict
description and teeth edging truth. Here was beauty
and here was nowhere. The smell of hurrying passed
my nostrils with the smell of sea water and fresh fish
wind, there was history which had taught my eyes to
look for escape even beneath the almond leaves fat
as women, the conch shell tiny as sand, the rock
stone old like water. I learned to read this from a
woman whose hand trembled at the past, then even
being born to her was temporary, wet and thrown half
dressed among the dozens of brown legs itching to
run. It was as if a signal burning like a fer de lance's
sting turned my eyes against the water even as love
for this nigger beach became resolute.

There it was anyway, some damn memory half-eaten
and half hungry. To hate this, they must have been
dragged through the Manzinilla spitting out the last
spun syllables for cruelty, new sound forming,
pushing toward lips made to bubble blood. This road
could match that. Hard-bitten on mangrove and wild
bush, the sea wind heaving any remnants of
consonant curses into choking aspirate. No
language is neutral seared in the spine's unravelling.
Here is history too. A backbone bending and
unbending without a word, heat, bellowing these
lungs spongy, exhaled in humming, the ocean, a
way out and not anything of beauty, tipping turquoise
and scandalous. The malicious horizon made us the
essential thinkers of technology. How to fly gravity,
how to balance basket and prose reaching for
murder. Silence done curse god and beauty here,
people does hear things in this heliconia peace
a morphology of rolling chain and copper gong
now shape this twang, falsettos of whip and air
rudiment this grammar. Take what I tell you. When
these barracks held slaves between their stone
halters, talking was left for night and hush was idiom
and hot core.

Pilate was that river I never crossed as a child. A woman, my mother, was weeping on its banks, weeping for the sufferer she would become, she a too black woman weeping, those little girls trailing her footsteps reluctantly and without love for this shaking woman blood and salt in her mouth, weeping, that river gushed past her feet blocked her flight ... and go where, lady, weeping and go where, turning back to face herself now only the oblique shape of something without expectation, her body composed in doubt then she'd come to bend her back, to dissemble, then to stand on anger like a ledge, a tilting house, the crazy curtain blazing at her teeth. A woman who thought she was human but got the message, female and black and somehow those who gave it to her were like family, mother and brother, spitting woman at her, somehow they were the only place to return to and this gushing river had already swallowed most of her, the little girls drowned on its indifferent bank, the river hardened like the centre of her, spinning chalk stone on its frill, burden in their slow feet, they weeping, she, *go on home*, in futility. There were dry-eyed cirri tracing the blue air that day. Pilate was that river I ran from leaving that woman, my mother, standing over its brutal green meaning and it was over by now and had become so ordinary as if not to see it any more, that constant veil over the eyes, the blood-stained blind of race and sex.

I walk Bathurst Street until it come like home
Pearl was near Dupont, upstairs a store one
christmas where we pretend as if nothing change we,
make rum punch and sing, with bottle and spoon,
song we weself never even sing but only hear when
we was children. Pearl, squeezing her big Point
Fortin self along the narrow hall singing *Drink a rum
and a* ... Pearl, working nights, cleaning, Pearl beating
books at her age, Pearl dying back home in a car
crash twenty years after everything was squeezed in,
a trip to Europe, a condominium, a man she suckled
like a baby. Pearl coaxing this living room with a
voice half lie and half memory, a voice no room
nowhere could believe was sincere. Pearl hoping this
room would catch fire above this frozen street. Our
singing parched, drying in the silence after the
chicken and ham and sweet bread effort to taste like
home, the slim red earnest sound of long ago with the
blinds drawn and the finally snow for christmas and
the mood that rum in a cold place takes. Well, even
our nostalgia was a lie, skittish as the truth these
bundle of years.

But wait, this must come out then. A hidden verb
takes inventory of those small years like a person
waiting at a corner, counting and growing thin
through life as cloth and as water, hush ... Look I
hated something, policemen, bankers, slavetraders,
shhh ... still do and even more these days. This city,
mourning the smell of flowers and dirt, cannot tell
me what to say even if it chokes me. Not a single
word drops from my lips for twenty years about living
here. Dumbfounded I walk as if these sidewalks are a
place I'm visiting. Like a holy ghost, I package the
smell of zinnias and lady of the night, I hoard the taste
of star apples and granadilla. I return to that once
grammar struck in disbelief. Twenty years. Ignoring
my own money thrown on the counter, the race
conscious landlords and their jim crow flats, oh yes!
here! the work nobody else wants to do ... it's good
work I'm not complaining! but they make it taste bad,
bitter like peas. You can't smile here, is a sin, you
can't play music, it too loud. There was a time I could
tell if rain was coming, it used to make me sad the
yearly fasting of trees here, I felt some pity for the
ground turned hot and cold. All that time taken up
with circling this city in a fever. I remember then, and
it's hard to remember waiting so long to live ... anyway
it's fiction what I remember, only mornings took a long
time to come, I became more secretive, language
seemed to split in two, one branch fell silent, the other
argued hotly for going home.

In another place, not here, a woman might touch
something between beauty and nowhere, back there
and here, might pass hand over hand her own
trembling life, but I have tried to imagine a sea not
bleeding, a girl's glance full as a verse, a woman
growing old and never crying to a radio hissing of a
black boy's murder. I have tried to keep my throat
gurgling like a bird's. I have listened to the hard
gossip of race that inhabits this road. Even in this I
have tried to hum mud and feathers and sit peacefully
in this foliage of bones and rain. I have chewed a few
votive leaves here, their taste already disenchanting
my mothers. I have tried to write this thing calmly
even as its lines burn to a close. I have come to know
something simple. Each sentence realised or
dreamed jumps like a pulse with history and takes a
side. What I say in any language is told in faultless
knowledge of skin, in drunkenness and weeping,
told as a woman without matches and tinder, not in
words and in words and in words learned by heart,
told in secret and not in secret, and listen, does not
burn out or waste and is plenty and pitiless and loves.

V i

Maybe this wide country just stretches your life to a thinness
just trying to take it in, trying to calculate in it what you must
do, the airy bay at its head scatters your thoughts like someone
going mad from science and birds pulling your hair, ice invades
your nostrils in chunks, land fills your throat, you are so busy
with collecting the north, scrambling to the Arctic so wilfully, so
busy getting a handle to steady you to this place you get blown
into bays and lakes and fissures you have yet to see, except
on a map in a schoolroom long ago but you have a sense that
whole parts of you are floating in heavy lake water heading for
what you suspect is some other life that lives there, and you, you
only trust moving water and water that reveals itself in colour. It
always takes long to come to what you have to say, you have to
sweep this stretch of land up around your feet and point to the
signs, pleat whole histories with pins in your mouth and guess
at the fall of words.

V ii

But the sight of land has always baffled you,
there is dirt somewhere older than any exile
and try as you might, your eyes only compose
the muddy drain in front of the humid almond
tree, the unsettling concrete sprawl of the housing
scheme, the stone your uncle used to smash his name
into another uncle's face, your planet is your hands,
your house behind your eyebrows and the tracing
paper over the bead of islands of indifferent and
reversible shapes, now Guadeloupe is a crab pinched
at the waist, now Nevis' borders change by mistake
and the carelessness of history, now sitting in Standard
Five, the paper shifting papery in the sweat of your
fingers you come to be convinced that these lines will
not matter, your land is a forced march on the bottom
of the Sargasso, your way tangled in life

V iii

I am giving up on land to light on, it's only true, it is only
something someone tells you, someone you should not trust
anyway. Days away, years before, a beer at your lips and the view
from Castara, the ocean as always pulling you towards its bone
and much later, in between, learning to drive the long drive
to Burnt River, where the land is not beautiful, braised
like the back of an animal, burnt in coolness, but the sky is,
like the ocean pulling you toward its bone, skin falling away
from your eyes, you see it without its history of harm, without
its damage, or everywhere you walk on the earth there's harm,
everywhere resounds. This is the only way you will know
the names of cities, not charmed or overwhelmed, all you see is
museums of harm and metros full, in Paris, walls inspected
crudely for dates, and Amsterdam, street corners full of
druggists, ashen with it, all the way from Suriname, Curaçao,
Dutch and German inking their lips, pen nibs of harm blued in
the mouth, not to say London's squares, blackened in statues,
Zeebrugge, searching the belly of fish, Kinshasa, through an
airplane window the dictator cutting up bodies grips the plane
to the tarmac and I can't get out to kiss the ground

V iv

This those slaves must have known who were my mothers, skin
falling from their eyes, they moving toward their own bone,
"so thank god for the ocean and the sky all implicated, all
unconcerned," they must have said, "or there'd be nothing to
love." How they spent a whole lifetime undoing the knot
of a word and as fast it would twirl up again, spent
whole minutes inching their eyes above sea level only
for latitude to shift, only for a horrible horizon to list, thank god
for the degrees of the chin, the fooling plane of a doorway, only
the mind, the not just simple business of return and turning,
that is for scholars and indecisive frigates, circling and circling,
stripped in their life, naked as seaweed, they would have sat
and sunk but no, the sky was a doorway, a famine and a jacket,
the sea a definite post

V v

I'm giving up on land to light on, slowly, it isn't land,
it is the same as fog and mist and figures and lines
and erasable thoughts, it is buildings and governments
and toilets and front door mats and typewriter shops,
cards with your name and clothing that comes undone,
skin that doesn't fasten and spills and shoes. It's paper,
paper, maps. Maps that get wet and rinse out, in my hand
anyway. I'm giving up what was always shifting, mutable
cities' fluorescences, limbs, chalk curdled blackboards
and carbon copies, wretching water, cunning walls. Books
to set it right. Look. What I know is this. I'm giving up.
No offence. I was never committed. Not ever, to offices
or islands, continents, graphs, whole cloth, these sequences
or even footsteps

V vi

Light passes through me lightless, sound soundless,
smoking nowhere, groaning with sudden birds. Paper
dies, flesh melts, leaving stockings and their useless vanity
in graves, bodies lie still across foolish borders.
I'm going my way, going my way gleaning shade, burnt
meridians, dropping carets, flung latitudes, inattention,
screeching looks. I'm trying to put my tongue on dawns
now, I'm busy licking dusk away, tracking deep twittering
silences. You come to this, here's the marrow of it, not
moving, not standing, it's too much to hold up, what I
really want to say is, I don't want no fucking country, here
or there and all the way back, I don't like it, none of it,
easy as that. I'm giving up on land to light on, and why not,
I can't perfect my own shadow, my violent sorrow, my
individual wrists.

III

That north burnt country ran me down
to the city, mordant as it is, the whole
terror of nights with yourself and what
will happen, animus, loose like that, sweeps
you to embrace its urban meter,
the caustic piss of streets,
you surrender your heart to a numb symmetry
of procedures, you study the metaphysics of
corporate instructions and not just,
besieged by now, the ragged, serrated theories
of dreams walking by, banked in sleep

that wild waiting at traffic lights off
the end of the world, where nothing is simple,
nothing, in the city there is no simple love
or simple fidelity, the heart is slippery,
the body convulsive with disguises
abandonments, everything is emptied,
wrappers, coffee cups, discarded shoes,
trucks, street corners, shop windows, cigarette
ends, lungs, ribs, eyes, love,
the exquisite rush of nothing,
the damaged horizon of skyscraping walls,
nights insomniac with pinholes of light

XII

It was late spring then, it was warm already,
he, jeremiad at the door holding the rough bible
to his temple like rhymed stone, she the last bolt
in her head shut, "Alan, let me pass."
"Oh my god!" his mother foretelling the meter,
he versed, "You're not leaving here with what is mine,"

her heart travelled the short distance of their joy
all the anger she had vaulted like gold belongings,
"Call the police! child, call the police! 911!"
The rake? The gloves? Had they come for the neighbours' things?
the tulip, the infinitesimal petals of spirea, the blossoms
he kissed this morning? "Here, wait." Then he would give them
their clippers, the branches of lilacs, the watering hose,
the two lengths of wild grasses that came off his hands.

They couldn't have come here to his house to stop him
from quarrelling with his own wife, it was the clippers
or the rake or their garden hose. He would straighten
things out, he would confess to the poppies, the white astilbe
Julia was leaving and no way she was taking what was his,
declaring the hedge clippers he said, "Look take it ..."

"What the devil ..." already descending.
"What the devil you all making so much noise for?"
then his chest flowered stigma of scarlet bergamot
their petal tips prickled his shirt, spread to his darkening
throat, he dropped the clippers to hold his breaking face,
he felt dry, "Jesus ... thirsty ..." he called, falling.

XIII

I don't remember that frail morning, how
could I? No one wakes up thinking of a stranger,
a life away, falling. I don't recall the
morning at all, as urgent or remarkable, though
falling was somehow predictable, but only when
you think of it later, falling is all you can do,
as hereditary as thirst, and so of course
he was thirsty, as I, craving a slake of baby's
breath, or bergamot, though we were not the same,
god would not be sufficient for me,
nor the ache and panic of a city surprising,
but thirst I know, and falling, thirst for fragrant
books, a waiting peace, for life, for just halting,
so I could breathe an air less rancid, live, anonymously

so no I don't recall the day, why would I? Let
alone, I've been busy with my own life, you have
to be on your toes or else you'll drown
in the thought of your own diminishing, as I said
I crave of course being human as he must have
and she, but not to let it get away with you,
don't dwell too long, don't stand still here,
I skim, I desert, I break of the edges,
I believe nothing, I dream but that's free

XV

All the hope gone hard. That is a city.
The blind houses, the cramped dirt, the broken
air, the sweet ugliness, the blissful and tortured
flowers, the misguided clothing, the bricked lies
the steel lies, all the lies seeping from flesh
falling in rain and snow, the weeping buses,
the plastic throats, the perfumed garbage, the
needled sky, the smogged oxygen, the deathly clerical
gentlemen cleaning their fingernails at the stock
exchange, the dingy hearts in the newsrooms, that is
a city, the feral amnesia of us all

XVII

It isn't, it really isn't
the city, brief as history,
but my life in it passing sooner
than this thirst is finished, I
can offer nothing except a few glances
an uneasy sleep, a wild keening,
it would appear nothing said matters,
nothing lived, but, this is my occupation.
One day I will record the tenses of light,
not now

XVIII

Around them the city is waking up as a girl vanishes
as light,
two women feel limbless, handless, motionless
what will they do now

It is only she that brings them to any life,
makes them
understand what day it is and that perhaps
things may pass

since that day which they are still standing in,
skinless.
Time starts with her and ends when she leaves
and even

if she vanishes on her bicycle of light,
when all
she is occupied with is fleeing them, they know
much more is gone

She will return to set them in motion, they hope
they will tell her,
they will confess their loneliness, they will
promise her

all the promises on their lips, to forget, to patch it
up, to carry on.
They will dream for her all the things people dream
for people they love

they will dream her first kiss, they will dream her
graduation from college,
they will dream her wedding, they will dream her children,
if only

she would turn around and look for them. Their eyes
are eager,
their hands waiting to smooth her wedding dress, to button
her satin shoes,

to pat her hair. They lust to kiss her husband,
to tell him
he must be careful with their girl, she's the only daughter
they have

they will love
his dark face, his even skin, his staggering smile.
She will turn
around they wish, each elated, each ready

they think
to make it right if only she does, to start anew.
They imagine each
that they will be ready with a rare laugh if she turns

and if she comes back
each plans to forgive the other, not to quibble
as to whom
she loves more or whom she smiles at first. They are breathless

for her
and they think that the picture of them standing there
must seem exultant
and deserving of her and without despair. They could both

attest
in that moment to representing branches and fire and flight.
Fleeing.
Is fleeing what the curve of her back means? Is there shrinking

The street begins
to move, and they are caught in an abrupt wind, the traffic
summing up
itself to its usual rush, the life around them pearls

against their grain
until they are stems on which dresses gust and fly, leaves
caught
in another time, in the middle of life they are an outskirt.

They've gathered all their fragile veins
and if only
she were to come back she would see them in full blood.
But to anyone walking

by, they are unslaked as ghosts.
They cannot summon hope though they are bursting with it,
it is so subterranean
it cannot break the surface of their skin, it cannot lap

their waiting arms
and overwhelm their failures, as it must
were she
to look back to their exact vision,

one solidly inconsolable, the other all dead flutter.
The street
now in full flight, no one notices that they are arrested,
waiting for a return

People bump against them, a murmured "sorry" cannot know
how appropriate it is,
an impatient brushing, cannot truly feel
their immobility

XXX

Spring darkness is forgiving. It doesn't descend
abruptly before you have finished work,
it approaches palely waiting for you
to get outside to witness another illumined hour

you feel someone brush against you,
on the street, you smell leather, the lake,
the coming leaves, the rain's immortality
pierces you, but you will be asleep when it arrives

you will lie in the groove of a lover's neck
unconscious, translucent, tendons singing,
and that should be enough, the circumference
of the world narrowed to your simple dreams

Days are perfect, that's the thing about them,
standing here in half darkness, I think this.
It's difficult to rise to that, but I expect it
I expect each molecule of my substance to imitate that

I can't of course, I can't touch syllables
tenderness, throats.
Look it's like this, I'm just like the rest,
limping across the city, flying when I can

One year she sat at the television weeping,
no reason,
the whole time

and the next, and the next

the wars' last and late night witness,
some she concluded are striving on grief
and burnt clothing, bloody rags, bomb-filled shoes

the pitiful domestic blankets
in the hospitals,
the bundles of plump
corpses waiting or embraced by screams,
the leaking chests and ridiculous legs

the abrupt density of life gone out, the
manifold substances of stillness

nothing personal is recorded here,
you must know that, but
one year the viciousness got to be too much

the news was advertisement for movies,
the movies were the real killings

the baked precipitous ditches,
twisted metal hulks of things that used to be,
fires intense as black holes, voids in schoolyards
and hotels, in kitchens and prophetic boys

all this became ordinary far from where it happened

the Arab faces were Arab faces after all,
not even the western hostages were hostages,
the lives of movie stars were more lamentable,
and the wreckage of streets was unimportant

what confidences would she tell you then,
what would possibly be safe in your hands

but never mind that, here is the latest watchful hour

– twenty-seven in Hillah, three in fighting in
Amariya, two by roadside bombing, Adhaim,
five by mortars in Afar, in firefight in Samarra

two, two in collision near Khallis, council member
in Kirkuk, one near medical complex, two in
Talafar, five by suicide bomb in Kirkuk, five

by suicide in Shorgat, one in attack on police
chief, Buhurz, five by car bomb in Baquba,
policeman in Mosul, two by car bomb, Madaen

five by mortars in Talafar, Sufi follower
near Baghdad, twelve by suicide bomb in
restaurant, bystander in Dora, in Mishada,
in Hillah, twenty-seven again, twenty-seven –

she's heard clearly now, twenty-three,
by restaurant bomb near green zone, Ibn Zanbour,
and so clear, syntonic, one, threading a needle

three beating dust from slippers, anyone looking
for a newspaper, an idea in their head like figs will soon
be in season, four playing dominoes, drinking Turkish coffee

seven by shop window, with small girl, in wading pool,
twelve half naked by river, nine shot dead in

Missouri shopping mall, possible yes, in restaurant
in Madison, three nephews, one aunt in Nashville fire bomb,
six by attack near hospital in Buffalo, two listening to radio

sixteen by bomb at football stadium, one reading
on bus "the heart is enclosed in a pericardial sac
that is lined with the parietal layers of serous membrane ..."

three with the electricity gone since Thursday,
still fumbling for candles then finding the matches

beating on the tympanic bone, by suicide bomb,
by suicide bomb, by car bomb, by ambush, any
number by sunlight, in daylight, by evening

still on those safe streets, amber alerts go out
by television, by puppetry, in sessions of paranoia,
in heavy suits with papers in cool hands as if staring at fools

there are announcements of imagined disturbances,
of dreads and sometimes it must be play, surely,
and the peculiar fragility of power

where it's the safest they use yellow and amber
and red pretending like the movies that there's
a bad guy every sixty seconds, and a car chase
coming and a hero with fire power

still in June,
in their hiatus eight killed by suicide bomb at
bus station, at least eleven killed in Shula at
restaurants, at least fifteen by car bomb, Irbil

At least someone should stay awake, she thinks,
someone should dream them along the abysmal roads

twenty-three by suicide bomb at Ibn Zanbour kebab
restaurant, no need to repeat this really, just the name
of the kebab place is new, isn't it

enough numbers still to come so twenty
outside bank in Kirkuk, the numbers so random,
so shapeless, apart from their shape, their seduction of infinity

the ganglia and meninges, the grey matter
of the cerebrum, the viscous peritoneal cavity

did she say two listening to the radio, to Nancy Amriq perhaps
any, any, preferring by sleep, by magic, in hallucinations

but here it is in rush hour, in traffic, a queue near the scarf
seller, in a moment's inattention, injured by petals of nails,
and hot wire, fugitive valves, a rain of small glittering teeth

and bones beatific, sharpened with heat, at least

it was sudden if not predictable at any rate
not on Sunset Boulevard, Potsdame Strasse,
Oxford Circus, Rue du Faubourg St. Honore and
all those streets

of reasonable suspicion, of self-fulfilling
dread, charred by home improvements,
self-makeovers, what goes for conscience now

what foundations, what animus calms, we're
doing the best we can with these people,
what undeniable hatred fuels them, what else
can we do, nothing but maim them,

we do not deserve it, it's out of the blue,
the sleeplessness at borders, the poor sunlight,
the paralyzed cars, they hate our freedom,

they want the abominable food from our mouths

"It is worst during the night
when the bombardment is most intense"

look, where are the matches, no, don't light a fire,
the tap's dripping precious,
the electricity will soon come back, how far
away is it now, the phosphorescent bodies,
the tremulous wounded hallways

she has to keep watch at the window
of the television, she hears what is never shown,
the details are triumphant,
she'll never be able to write them in time

the paper now, and where's the hair oil,
the butter's gone rancid,
remember that cat we used to have,
it disappeared the first day,
lemons, remember to buy lemons

there's another life, she listens, each hour, each night,
behind the flat screen and the news anchor,
the sleek, speeding cars, the burgers, the breaking

celebrity news, unrealities of faraway islands,
bickering and spiteful,
each minute so drastic, they win a million dollars

the waiting, she can't bear the waiting,
the metal, metal, metal of waiting,
she sits devoted, the paring knife close
to a harvest of veins

now everything is in her like ends and tastes,
the loosening clasp of affinities
everyone grows perversely accustomed,
she refuses

If they're numb over there, and all around her,
she'll gather the nerve endings
spilled on the streets, she'll count them like rice grains

she'll keep them for when they're needed

for music and the ornaments of air without bombing,
for bread and honey, the kilos of figs
in December and baked yams from burnt

fingered vendors, the washing to be done,
the sewing, the bicycles to be repaired,
the daily lists to be made of mundane
matters, like the cost of sugar, or the girl losing
her new pencils again

and not to say, for the memories of the forgetful, the
spinners of silences,
the teethed impasto of broadcasts

she'll gather the passions of women,
their iron feet, their bitter hair, their
perpetual nuptial assignment

to battered kitchens and rooms
radiant with their blood vessels

their waiting at doors
at night in the universe, such waiting

the mind surpasses, the bones are a failure,
the pregnancies wretched again, and again

she'll store the nerves' endings in glass
coloured bottles on a tree near the doorsteps,
for divine fierce years to come

when the planet is ruined, the continent
forlorn in water and smoke

till then
where are the packages of black pepper,
the oil for the lilac bore, the shovel

if she wakes up tomorrow and things are still this way,
then the shovel for the ice
in the garden, the winter-eaten sidewalk

someone died leaving her a basket,
she'll fill it with the overflow,
line it with day lilies and the wine
she makes sitting there
pressing and pressing these bundles of dried blooms

the bus stations are empty and sobbing,
the unemployment lines are runny
like broken eggs, the construction sites
pile up endlessly, nothing is finished

she is a woman who is losing the idea
of mathematics,
the maximum is so small, the
crushed spines of vehicles fly in the air,
all September, all October

where's the flour, the nighttime stories, where's
the sugar for the tongue's amusement, muscle
and likeness,

now she wishes she could hear
all that noise that poets make about
time and timelessness

come throw some water on her forehead,
look for the butterflies so wingless,
the oven is freezing with a steady, steady cold

Afterword

Maps

An oral ruttier is a long poem containing navigational instructions which sailors learned by heart and recited from memory. The poem contained the routes and tides, the stars and maybe the taste and flavour of the waters, the coolness, the saltiness; all for finding one's way at sea. Perhaps, too, the reflection and texture of the sea bed, also the sight of birds, the direction of their flight. This and an instrument called a Kamal which measured the altitude of stars from the horizon.

It was said in my family that my grandfather was part Carib. The parts of my grandfather which were part Carib were his cheekbones, which were high, not in an African-high way but in a square flat way—a Carib-high way. Then there was the tawny hue sometimes visible under the dark brown of his skin. Then the occasional straightness of regions of hair on his head. The rest of my grandfather, his height, the remaining territories of his hair, the dominant colour of his skin, the majority of him, was African. There were, too, indefinite parts of him which either hegemony could claim. But there was no war, there never had been, both had settled calmly in my grandfather.

Ruttier for the Marooned in the Diaspora

Marooned, tenantless, deserted. Desolation castaway, abandoned in the world. They was, is, wandered, wanders as spirits who dead cut, banished, seclude, refuse, shut the door, derelict, relinquished, apart. More words she has left them. Cast behind. From time to time they sit on someone's bed or speak to someone in the ear and that is why someone steps out of rhythm; that is why someone drinks liquor or trips or shuts or opens a door out of nowhere. All unavailable to themselves, open to the world, cut in air. They disinherit answers. They owe, own nothing. They whisper every so often and hear their own music in churches, restaurants, hallways, all paths, between fingers and lips, between cars and precipices, and the weight of themselves in doorways, on the legs of true hipsters, guitars and bones for soup, veins.

Excerpted from Dionne Brand, *A Map to the Door of No Return: Notes to Belonging* (Toronto: Vintage Canada, 2000).

And it doesn't matter where in the world, this spirit is no citizen, no national, no one who is christened, no sex, this spirit is washed of all this lading, bag and baggage, jhaji bundle, georgie bindle, lock stock, knapsack, and barrel, and only holds its own weight which is nothing, which is memoryless and tough with remembrances, heavy with lightness, aching with grins. They wander as if they have no century, as if they can bound time, as if they can sit in a café in Brugge just as soon as smoke grass in Tucson, Arizona, and chew coca in the high Andes for coldness.

Pays for everything this one, hitchhikes, dies in car accidents, dresses in Hugo Boss and sings ballads in Catholic churches, underwater rum shops. This is a high-wire spirit laden with anchors coming in to land, devoluting heirlooms, parcels, movable of nips, cuts, open secrets of foundlings, babes, ignitions, strips of water, cupfuls of land, real estates of ocean floors and steaming asphalt streets, meat of trees and lemons, bites of Communion bread and chunks of sky, subdivisions of stories.

These spirits are tenants of nothing jointly, temporary inheritors of pages 276 and 277 of an old paleology. They sometimes hold a life like a meeting in a detention camp, like a settlement without a stone or stick, like dirty shelves, like a gag in the mouth. Their dry goods are all eaten up already and their hunger is tenacious. This spirit doubling and quadrupling, resuming, skipping stairs and breathing elevators is possessed with uncommunicated undone plots; consignments of compasses whose directions tilt, skid off known maps, details skitter off like crabs. This spirit abandoned by all mothers, fathers, all known progenitors, rents rooms that disappear in its slate stone wise faces. These people un-people, de-people until they jump overboard, hijack buildings and planes. They disinhabit unvisited walls. They unfriend friends in rye and beer and homemade wine and forties.

She undwells solitudes, liquors' wildernesses. This drunk says anything, cast away in his foot ship, retired from the world. This whisperer, sprawler, mincer, deaconess, soldier is marooning, is hungering, is unknowing. This one in the suit is a litigant in another hearing gone in the world. This spirit inhaling cigarettes is a chain along a thousand glistening moss harbours and spends nights brooding and days brooding and afternoons watching the sea even at places with no harbours and no sea. This one is gone, cast off and wandering wilfully. This is intention as well as throwaway. This is deliberate and left. Slipstream and sailing. Deluge. These wander anywhere, clipping shirt-tails and hems and buying shoes and vomiting. These shake with dispossession and bargain, then change their minds. They get trapped in houses one minute, just as anybody can, and the next they break doorways and sit in company mixing up the talk with crude honesty and lies. Whatever is offered or ceded is not the thing, not enough, cannot grant their easement, passports to unknowing everything.

This spirit's only conveyance is each morning, breath, departures of any kind, tapers, sheets of anything, paper, cloth, rain, ice, spittle, glass. It likes blue and fireflies. Its face is limpid. It has the shakes, which is how it rests and rests cutting oval shells of borders with jagged smooth turns. It is an oyster leaving pearl. These spirits have lived in any given year following the disaster, in any given place. They have visited shutters and doors and thermal glass windows looking for themselves. They are a prism of endless shimmering colour. If you sit with them they burn and blister. They are bony with hope, muscular with grief possession.

Marooned on salted highways, in high grass, on lumpy beds, in squares with lights, in knowledge plantations and cunning bridges grasping two cities at the same time. Marooned in the mouth where things escape before they are said, are useless before they are given or echo. Marooned in realms of drift, massacres of doubt, implications. Marooned where the body burns with long-ing for everything and nothing, where it circles unable to escape a single cen-tury; tenements and restagings of alien, new landings. Marooned in outcropping, up-crops of cities already abandoned for outposts in suburbs. Deserted in the fragility of concrete rooms, the chalked clammy dust of dry walls, the rot of sewer pipes and the blanket of city grates.

Marooned in music, dark nightclubs of weeping, in never-sufficient verses, uncommunicated sentences, strict tears, in copper throats. Where days are prisons this spirit is a tenant. She moves along incognito on foot, retreating into unknowing, retreating into always orphanages, dew light, paradise, eclipses, bruised skies, atomic stars, an undeviating ever.

So if now and then they slump on beds in exhaustion it is hallowed pain. If they sink in the ear it is subversions that change their minds even before they are deployed, unexpected architectures of ambivalent longing, cargoes of wilderness. It is their solitudes' wet desolations. If they finger a string across a piece of wood and a tremolo attacks a room, toccata erupt, coloratura saturate the walls, it is their lost and found dereliction. If virtuosity eludes them, relin-quishes them, cast away to themselves only, gaping limbs and topographies, it is just as much spiritoso, madrigal, mute chirping, ululating twilight unvisiting.

It is now and she, they whisper in Walkmans, in cities' streets with two mil-lion people gazing at advertisements. It is now and he, they run his fingers over a moustache flicking frost away, breathing mist like a horse. Cities and public squares and public places corral their gifts of imagined suns and imag-ined families, where they would have been and who they might have been and when. Cities make them pause and wonder at what they might have thought had it been ever, and had it been dew light and had it been some other shore, and had it been time in their own time when now they are out of step with themselves as spirits are. Electric lights and neon and cars' metal humming convince them of cultivated gateways and generations of water, of necessities they cannot put back together. Their coherence is incoherence, provocations of scars and knives and paradise, of tumbling wooden rivers and liquid hills.

More Maps

According to my grandmother, the world was the house, its perimeter its shadow which the sun made each morning to the back of the house, withdrew at midday, and refigured in the afternoon in the front yard. Her bed was the ship of the world and her broom was her harpoon to spear us when we reached beyond its boundaries. She sailed in that bed, sending signals to the grocery store, written on brown paper bags. One pound red beans, ten pounds rice, five pounds sugar, two pounds salt fish, four pounds split peas, ten cents worth of oil, one-half pound lard; on copy book leaves in her rickety writing she ordered the shopkeeper, "Dear Lloyd, please trust me these goods, until …"

   She sent children in directions she herself never arrived at. She only navigated and travelled the seven windows of the house, and the two doorways.

—Dionne Brand

Acknowledgements

From *No Language Is Neutral*
Toronto: McClelland & Stewart, 1998
> No language is neutral
> There it was anyway, some damn memory half-eaten
> Pilate was that river I never crossed as a child
> I walk Bathurst Street until it come like home
> But wait, this must come out then
> In another place, not here, a woman might touch

From *Land to Light On*
Toronto: McClelland & Stewart, 1997
> V i
> V ii
> V iii
> V iv
> V v
> V vi

From *thirsty*
Toronto: McClelland & Stewart, 2002
> III
> XII
> XIII
> XV
> XVII
> XVIII
> XXX

From *Inventory*
Toronto: McClelland & Stewart, 2006
> III
>> One year she sat at the television weeping
>> nothing personal is recorded here

what confidences would she tell you then
she's heard clearly now, twenty-three
beating on the tympanic bone, by suicide bomb
At least someone should stay awake, she thinks
and bones beatific, sharpened with heat, at least
"It is worst during the night
there's another life, she listens, each hour, each night
If they're numb over there, and all around her
she'll gather the passions of women
till then / where are the packages of black pepper
she is a woman who is losing the idea